Flute

Globetrotters

12 pieces in styles from around the world

Ros Stephen

MUSIC DEPARTMENT

OXFORD

UNIVERSITY PRESS

OXFORD
UNIVERSITY PRESS

Great Clarendon Street, Oxford OX2 6DP, England

Oxford University Press is a department of the University of Oxford.
It furthers the University's aim of excellence in research, scholarship,
and education by publishing worldwide

1 3 5 7 9 10 8 6 4 2

ISBN 978-0-19-337685-4

Music and text origination by Julia Bovee
Printed in Great Britain on acid-free paper by
Halstan & Co. Ltd., Amersham, Bucks.

All the tunes in this book are original pieces by Ros Stephen.

Author acknowledgements: Ros would like to thank Julian Rowlands, Philip Croydon, Laura Jones,
and all the musicians who played on the CD. Nicky would like to thank Andrew King
and the flautists of Badminton and Dean Close schools.

CD credits: Nicky King (flute), Javier Fioramonti (guitar), Pete Rosser (accordion),
Yaron Stavi and Tom Mason (double bass), Jonathan Taylor (piano), Andrew Tween (drums/percussion),
Philip Bagenal (recording and mixing engineer), Andi Johnson (recording engineer)

Contents

Take a light-hearted trip around the world with this collection of 12 fun, original pieces. Suitable for flute players of 2+ years' experience (around grade 2 to 4 standard), the pieces are based on a wide variety of world-music styles.

Each piece comes with background information about the musical style and warm-up exercises to help with the specific demands of the music.

The accompanying CD includes authentic performance and play-along tracks for each piece, with a band comprising world-music specialists.

Flute accompaniment parts, suitable for a more advanced player or teacher, are provided for every piece, and piano accompaniments (with guitar chord symbols) for printing are included on the CD as PDFs. PC users can access the PDFs by selecting 'Computer' from the start-up menu and right-clicking on the CD drive to open the CD. Mac users should double-click on the data disc that appears when the CD is inserted to see the PDF files.

performance 1; backing 13

1. Guanabara Bay

Medium bossa nova ♩ = 108–112

mp
On a star-lit night we walk__ on Gua-na-ba-ra Bay__ while the

o-cean gent-ly whis-pers on the sand.__   **A** *mf* A sam-ba band is play-

-ing; mu-sic takes our cares a-way.__ *mp* I hope it ne-ver ends,

the mu-sic ne-ver ends.__ **B** *mf* In the ci-ty there are peo-

-ple danc-ing in the square   to a bos-sa no-va tune

mf **C** that's played so sweet-ly on gui-tar,__ and the rhy-thm of the sam-

-ba ech-oes through the warm night air.__ *mp* From Ri-o

poco rall. *p* I'll ne-ver go far.__

A piano accompaniment for printing is included on the CD (see page 3).

Flute accompaniment

Medium bossa nova ♩ = 108–112

2. Shanghai Rickshaw Ride

A piano accompaniment for printing is included on the CD (see page 3).

One of the most widely used flutes in traditional Chinese music is the *dizi* flute, which is made of bamboo and has a range of two and a half octaves. It has an extra hole covered by a very thin bamboo membrane; this resonates as the flute is played, creating a distinctive nasal, buzzing sound. Make sure you move your thumb and first finger together for the mordents (⋙) four and five bars before letter C, and remember to move your thumb onto the B♭ key for the mordent in the next bar. To avoid longer notes going flat, push your jaw forward slightly to end them, while maintaining diaphragm support.

Flute accompaniment

ossia: play at written octave

sub = subito

⊙performance 3; backing 15

3. Dancing in Odessa

Globetrotters
KLEZMER, E. EUROPE

A piano accompaniment for printing is included on the CD (see page 3).

Klezmer is Jewish music from eastern Europe and is characterized by expressive melodies, usually in minor keys, set against a strongly rhythmic accompaniment. Odessa is a town in Ukraine, famous for its Jewish cultural heritage. The flute was often used in the klezmer bands of the late nineteenth and early twentieth centuries, along with instruments such as the violin, clarinet, accordion, and double bass or tuba. This piece is a *freylekhs* (pronounced 'fray-lacks', a Yiddish word meaning joyful), which is a fast dance piece. It should be played energetically with a big sound and strong accents. Warm-up 3a will help you with the accents.

Flute accompaniment

9

4. 'Hole in my Shoe' Blues

Medium swing ♩ = 108

I've got a hole in my shoe,__ oh yeah! I've got a hole in my shoe,__ oh no!__ Well,

I've been walk-ing,__ walk-ing since the ear-ly morn-ing hours; now my sock is wet, what shall I do?__

I'm gon-na have to hop all the way to New Or-leans, oh poor me, I feel so blue.

A

I lost my mo-ney and my bus pass ex-pired. My bag is hea-vy and my legs are so tired.

Will I ev-er get there? Who knows? But if I do I will mend this shoe, that is for sure.

I'll get to New Or-leans some-how; some day I'll make it to your door.__

B

I've got a hole in my shoe,_ oh yeah! I've got a hole in my shoe,_ oh no!__ Well, I've been walk-ing,

walk-ing since the ear-ly morn-ing hours; now my sock is wet, what shall I do?__ I'm gon-na have to

molto rall.

hop all the way to New Or-leans, all I need is one new shoe, new shoe! Yeah!

A piano accompaniment for printing is included on the CD (see page 3).

The blues is a music of African-American origin dating back to the early twentieth century. It has had a strong influence on Western popular music, forming the roots of jazz, rhythm and blues, and rock. Blues songs are often sad, telling stories of hard lives, lost love, and misfortunes. This piece should be played with a 'swing' feel, which means pairs of quavers are played as an uneven long-short rhythm (♫ becomes ♪). Listen to the recording (track 4) to hear how this is done, then try saying the words along with the recording. For a further sense of style, listen to the jazz flautists Herbie Mann and Yusef Lateef.

Flute accompaniment

Gāyakī (singing style) ♩ = 80

No piano accompaniment is provided for this piece.

*There is a two-bar introduction on the CD backing track.

This piece is based on a South Indian Carnatic song form called a *kriti*. *Kritis* are usually made up of three sections: *pallavi* (a kind of refrain), *anupallavi* (first verse), and *charanam* (second and longest verse, often followed by an improvisation). Indian music uses ragas instead of scales; the raga specifies the notes to be used in a piece as well as other details such as ornamentation (*gamaka*), mood, or even the time of day when it should be played. This piece uses the Sarasangi raga (see Warm-up 5a). Carnatic music is traditionally played on a bamboo flute called a *venu*, accompanied by a drone instrument, called a *tambura*, and a *mridangam* drum. The Kaveri river is one of India's major rivers.

Flute accompaniment

Gāyakī (singing style) ♩ = 80

*There is a two-bar introduction on the CD backing track.

13

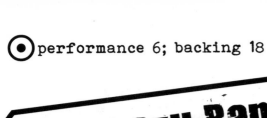

performance 6; backing 18

6. Iguazu Rapids

A piano accompaniment for printing is included on the CD (see page 3).

© Oxford University Press 2010 and 2012. Photocopying this copyright material is ILLEGAL.

The Iguazu river is on the Argentinian-Brazilian border and has some of the biggest waterfalls in the world. This piece is based on a style of folk music called *chamamé* that comes from North Eastern Argentina. Traditionally performed on accordion and guitar, *chamamé* is characteristically warm-hearted and upbeat music; for a flavour, listen to leading exponents Chango Spasiuk and Transito Cocomarola. In this piece the left hand of the piano is playing in 3/4 time while the melody is in 6/8 time; this is an example of polyrhythmic music (polyrhythmic means playing more than one rhythm at a time). See Warm-up 6a for help with these rhythms.

Flute accompaniment

Globetrotters
ARGENTINA

7. Tango in San Telmo

Slow milonga ♩ = 88

A piano accompaniment for printing is included on the CD (see page 3).

Tango comes from Argentina, and San Telmo is a famous district of Buenos Aires where you can see people dancing the tango at almost any time of the day or night. A *milonga* is a style of tango music and is also the term for a social tango dance. A traditional-style *milonga* is fast and lively, but this piece, influenced by the late twentieth-century 'nuevo tango' music of Astor Piazzolla, is slow and, like much tango music, rather sad. It should be played expressively with vibrato and a sweet tone. Listen to Astor Piazzolla's 'Histoire du Tango' (for flute and guitar) to hear the 'nuevo tango' style.

Flute accompaniment

Globetrotters
IRELAND

A piano accompaniment for printing is included on the CD (see page 3).

This tune is an Irish-style jig. Jigs are written in compound time, in this case 6/8, which means there are two dotted-crotchet beats (♩. ♩.) or two groups of three quavers (♫♪ ♫♪) per bar. Try saying 'one-and-a, two-and-a' to get the feel of the 6/8 rhythm. Irish flute players traditionally use a simple-system wooden instrument and add a lot of ornamentation to the music, giving it a very distinctive, rhythmic character. Make sure you play the ornaments crisply and quickly, and remember to use the second trill key for the mordents (∿) at letters B and C (see Warm-up 8b).

Flute accompaniment

19

9. Greenmarket Square

Globetrotters
SOUTH AFRICA

Joyful township swing ♩ = c.112

Oh yeah, the sun is a-shin-ing, let's do some shop-ping at Green-mar-ket Square to - day.___ We'll___ buy some sweet, jui-cy man-gos and tas-ty peach-es, oh let's go there right a - way.___ Oh yeah, we're walk-ing a - long, hear our song, yeah we're walk-ing a - long chew-ing bil - tong. Tastes pret-ty strange, we don't care 'cos we're hav-ing such fun __ at Green-mar-ket Square. Green-mar - - - ket Square_ is where_ they sell such sweet, jui-cy man-gos, de - li - cious peach - es, and all sorts of spi - ces too.___ We'll buy some ost - rich and ku-du, some boere-wors and beans, and cook them up in a stew.___

A piano accompaniment for printing is included on the CD (see page 3).

This is in the style of township jazz, which originated in the urban townships of South Africa in the mid twentieth century. This joyful, upbeat music is a fusion of American swing and traditional South African music, particularly kwela, and is often played on penny whistle or flute and accompanied by guitar, piano, drums, and bass. Two leading exponents of this style are Donald Kachamba and Barney Rachabane (who has collaborated with Hugh Masekela and Abdullah Ibrahim). Keep the tonguing action light to give this piece a laid-back summertime feel, but stay rhythmic; try practising with a metronome to make sure you don't slow down. Warm-up 9a will help you with the swing rhythm.

Flute accompaniment

10. Cairo Cradle Song

With expression ♩ = 80

A piano accompaniment for printing is included on the CD (see page 3).

This tune is in the style of an Arabic lullaby, and should be played very gently and sweetly with some vibrato. The traditional Egyptian ney flute is one of the oldest musical instruments still in use; it can even be seen in wall paintings in the pyramids. Made from a seven-segment piece of cane, it is end-blown and has a mellow and husky tone. It has a range of over three octaves; harmonics are used to reach the second and third octaves. You'll play some harmonics in this piece at letter A and two bars before letter B; Warm-up 10a will help you with these.

Flute accompaniment

11. Bulgarian Gallop

Lively and rhythmic ♩ = 132

Fred the horse has got two old wood-en legs; if you sing he'll do a cra-zy gal-lop-ing dance.

When he runs he makes a ter-ri-ble noise; you can hear him all the way from Ple-ven to France.

If you're mad e-nough to ride on his back, he will jump and spin and sing a ve-ry rude song.

If you're mad e-nough to ride on his back, he will throw you off un-less you're ev-er so strong.

Clack-e-ty bang, bang, clack-e-ty bang, bang, clack-e-ty bang go his two wood-en legs, it's a

bit of a bump-y, bit of a bump-y, bit of a bump-y ride! Try not to fall off, hold on tight,

try not to fall off, hold on tight, try not to fall off, hold on tight, you'll be all right! Try not to fall off,

hold on tight, try not to fall off, hold on tight, try not to fall off, hold on tight, oh, what a sight!_

A piano accompaniment for printing is included on the CD (see page 3).

*There is a four-bar introduction in the piano accompaniment and on the CD backing track.

© Oxford University Press 2010 and 2012. Photocopying this copyright material is ILLEGAL.

Bulgaria has a strong folk tradition: singing and dancing used to be common forms of village entertainment. The flute traditionally used in Bulgaria is the chromatic, end-blown *kaval* flute. It's usually made of wood, but can also be made from water buffalo horn. Bulgarian music is famous for its uneven rhythms, formed from combinations of two- and three-count beats. In this piece the seven quavers are divided into three groups: a slow unit of three quavers (♪♪♪) and two quick units of two quavers (♪♪ ♪♪). Use Warm-up 11a to learn the rhythms, then practise saying the words along with the recording (track 11). The ornaments should be played as mordents (𝄿).

Flute accompaniment

*There is a four-bar introduction in the piano accompaniment and on the CD backing track.

performance 12; backing 24*

12. White Nights in Narvik

Globetrotters
NORWAY

A piano accompaniment for printing is included on the CD (see page 3).

*Listen for the two-bar drum cue into letters B and D when playing along with the backing track.

© Oxford University Press 2012. Photocopying this copyright material is ILLEGAL.

7. Tango in San Telmo

Ros Stephen

D
p
mf
Am E7 Am F Am/E Am F Am/E E/G♯ F° E
E/G♯ F° E Gm6 Gm7/F E° Gm6 Gm7/F E° D D9/E D/A
E
mp
D D9/E D/A Dm9 Dm9/E Dm/A Dm Dm9/E Dm/A Am/C Dm9 Am/C Dm9 Am/C
rall.
B⌀ E7 Am F Am/E Am F Am/E Am
freely
3
Ped.

Narvik is a town in the north of Norway, inside the Arctic Circle, where for several weeks during summer the sun never sets. The flute traditionally used in Nordic folk music is the willow flute, or *seljefløyte*. It's an overtone flute with a fipple mouthpiece (like a recorder) and no finger holes. Notes are produced by covering and uncovering the end of the flute with the index finger of the right hand and varying the force of the air to get different notes in the harmonic series. The scale produced by these overtones is quite different from a standard Western scale; try it out in Warm-up 12b.

Flute accompaniment

Warm-up exercises

Although this book is written for the classical Western flute, many of the styles represented belong to older traditional instruments. To hear these instruments being played, search online for the following: Kevin Crawford (Irish wooden flute); Hans Fredrik Jacobsen (Norwegian willow flute); Kudsi Erguner (Arabic *ney* flute); Yu Xunfa (Chinese *dizi* flute); Theodosii Spassov (Bulgarian *kaval* flute); and Dr Natesan Ramani (South Indian *venu*).

1. Guanabara Bay

(a) BREATHING PRACTICE

In this piece you'll need to take a big, deep breath before each phrase. Remember to support the sound from the diaphragm. To increase your breathing capacity and diaphragm control, practise a series of five notes (B is a good one to start with), taking a quick, deep breath between each one (as if someone has just given you a fright). Drop your jaw as you breathe in. Try to make each note as long as possible—see if you can make the last note as long as the first one.

quick, deep breaths; don't stop!

see how long you can make this note last

(b) PHRASING AND TONGUING

This piece should sound smooth and relaxed; each phrase should ideally be played in one breath. Play this exercise with your metronome set to ♩ = 108. How many bars can you play in one breath? Can you manage more than the four written here? When this sounds really good, try it again, this time tonguing the notes. The tonguing should be very gentle: '*dah dah dah*' instead of '*te te te*'. Try to make it sound almost as smooth as it does with a slur; don't stop the air between notes.

2. Shanghai Rickshaw Ride

Brazil / China

(a) PENTATONIC SCALES

Traditional Chinese music is based on pentatonic (5-note) scales. Try playing the two pentatonic scales used in this piece:

D minor pentatonic scale

D major pentatonic scale

(b) ACTIVITY IDEAS

- The black notes on a piano form a pentatonic scale. Try making up a tune on the piano just using these notes; it's easy, even if you don't play the piano. Hold down the sustaining pedal and listen to the sound.
- Make up your own pentatonic melody on your flute using the notes of one of the scales above.

3. Dancing in Odessa

(a) ACCENTED NOTES

This piece should be very rhythmic and the accents played quite strongly. Make sure you use your diaphragm as well as your tongue to play the accents. If you're not sure how to do this, try saying 'woof' loudly. Put your hand on your diaphragm and feel it move. For the next exercise, play the first three bars without any tonguing, just using the diaphragm (think: 'ha ha ha'), then add the tonguing. When this is confident, try adding the accents.

(b) BULGAR RHYTHM

The *bulgar rhythm* is a quick 3–3–2 rhythmic pattern often heard in klezmer music. You'll play it three times in this piece; see if you can spot where. Try clapping the rhythm while saying the words.

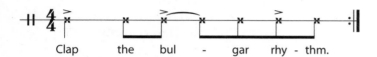

4. 'Hole in my Shoe' Blues

(a) SWING RHYTHM AND C BLUES SCALE

In *Ex. i* the swing quavers (♪) are written out as triplets, which is the closest way of notating their *long-short* rhythm. They aren't written like this in the piece because it would make the music hard to read, so you have to remember to play all the quavers with this rhythm. Using CD track 25 as a backing, play the swing rhythm on a single note to start with, thinking of the words as you play, then play a C blues scale (*Ex. ii*) with the same rhythm. Be careful not to hurry; swing should sound relaxed and laid-back.

Ex. i

Ex. ii

(b) IMPROVISING

Blues music, like jazz, often contains improvisation. Improvisation means making up your own tune on the spur of the moment. Start off by playing the C blues scale shown above. Then think of a simple four-bar question-and-answer phrase like 'Who can play a blues tune on their flute? I can play a blues tune on my flute.' Pick a note from the scale and try playing the rhythm of your phrase; when this feels easy, pick a different note. Then try using more than one note, or a different rhythm. Now you're improvising! Mix the notes up; they will sound great in any order. When this feels confident, try improvising along to CD track 25. Try to keep your improvisation simple and very rhythmic.

5. Kaveri Kriti

(a) SARASANGI RAGA

A raga is a selection of notes (like a scale) used to compose melodies in Indian classical music. This piece uses the Sarasangi raga (see below). Try playing it (don't worry if you find the low C a bit tricky; you don't have to play it in the piece).

Sarasangi raga

(b) IMPROVISING

Indian classical musicians often include long improvisations in performance; they improvise using the notes of the raga that the piece is based on. Try improvising along to CD track 26. To start with, play the raga shown in Ex. 5(a). Then pick three notes from the raga and play them using a simple rhythm. Try out some different notes and different rhythms. Next, ask a friend or your teacher to play along with you. Using your three notes, play a simple two-bar phrase such as:

Ask the other player to repeat your phrase after you've played it. Then ask them to make up a phrase using the same notes but in a different order or with a different rhythm and see if you can copy it. Take it in turns to make up a phrase, and see if you can make the rhythms gradually more complicated. When this feels easy, try adding another note or two from the raga.

(c) COMPOSE YOUR OWN INDIAN MELODY

On manuscript paper, try writing your own *anupallavi* section (the eight-bar section starting at letter 'A') using the notes of the Sarasangi raga.

6. Iguazu Rapids

(a) RHYTHM EXERCISES

Chamamé melodies often move between two- and three-beat rhythmic patterns, and a two-against-three rhythm is often heard in the accompaniment. Clap the rhythmic patterns below, with your metronome.

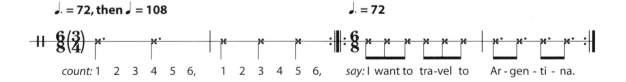

(b) TONGUING EXERCISES

The semiquavers (♪) in this piece can be played using either single or double tonguing. Practise your tonguing using the exercise below. Start off with single tonguing; when this feels easy, have a go at double tonguing using 'te-ke' (or 'de-ge'). Try to use as little tongue movement as possible so you don't interrupt the airflow.

7. Tango in San Telmo

(a) TONE CONTROL

Listen very carefully to your tuning and tonal quality in this exercise. Move your jaw back slightly for low notes and forward for high notes; the bigger the interval, the more you move your jaw. To get the feel of this, put the palm of your hand in front of your face and blow up and down your hand without moving your head. Start the following exercise slowly and gradually build up speed. Practise both tongued and slurred.

(b) NOTE ENDINGS

To prevent the last notes of phrases from going flat, push your jaw forward slightly to end them while maintaining diaphragm support. The following exercise will help you with this:

8. Dublin Time

(a) ARTICULATION

Start these exercises slowly, with your metronome set to ♩. = c.60; gradually speed up to ♩. = 84.

Ex. i

Ex. ii

(b) ORNAMENTS

The ornaments in this piece should be played as quickly as possible. Try playing them slowly then quickly, as shown in the examples below. Use the second trill key to play the Ds in *Ex. ii*. See if you can find some other places in the piece to play ornaments.

Ex. i   *Ex. ii*   *Ex. iii*

9. Greenmarket Square

(a) D MAJOR SWING

This tune is in the style of township swing. See Ex. 4(a) for an explanation of swing rhythm, then try clapping swing quavers along with CD track 9. When this feels confident, try playing the D major scale below with swing rhythm. Practise with both tongued and slurred quavers.

(b) RHYTHM EXERCISE

This exercise will help you count through the rests at letter 'B'. Start off by playing the extra Ds (written as small notes), then leave them out, but still think of the words as you play.

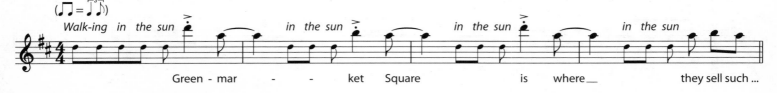

31

10. Cairo Cradle Song

(a) HARMONICS

The notes at letter 'A' of this piece are harmonics; they are the first notes in the harmonic series. Play them using the fingering for the lower octave (the notes written as diamonds) and overblow to reach the octave above for an authentic Egyptian sound!

overblow using the fingering for the lower octave

(b) HARMONIC SERIES

For fun, try out some more notes in the harmonic series. If you're not sure you're on the right note, check the pitch by playing it with the usual fingering. You can go even higher if you dare!

11. Bulgarian Gallop

(a) 7/8 RHYTHMIC PATTERNS

Clap these 7/8 rhythmic patterns along with CD track 11, saying the words as you clap. Notice how the quavers (♪) are always grouped in a 3-2-2 pattern. When this feels confident, try clapping the rhythm of the first four bars of the piece.

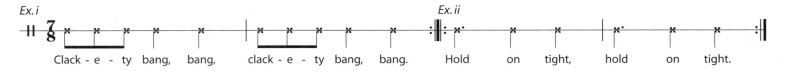

(b) HIJAZ MAQAM

The *Hijaz Maqam* scale is a characteristic scale often found in Bulgarian and Middle Eastern music. Try it out for a truly Eastern flavour!

12. White Nights in Narvik

(a) PLAYING QUICKLY

The ending of this piece should be played as fast as possible! To build up speed, play these exercises quite slowly at first, with your metronome set to ♩ = *c.*100, then gradually increase the tempo until you reach the fastest speed you can manage. See if you can go a bit faster each time you practise. Keep your fingers relaxed and close to their keys. When you get really good at this, try out some different articulations, for example slurring the first two quavers (♪) in each group. In the last exercise, be sure to lift your left-hand 1st finger when you play the D.

(b) OVERTONE SCALE

The overtone scale, or acoustic scale, contains notes from the harmonic series; this is the only scale you can play on a traditional Scandinavian willow flute. It can also be heard in the theme tune for *The Simpsons*!